Waterproof VICTORIAN FISH GUIDE

by Frank Prokop

Illustrations by Trevor Hawkins
Rigs by Geoff Wilson

ALBACORE

Scientific name: *Thunnus alalunga*. Also known as Tuna (Chicken of the sea).

Description: A common species of offshore waters. Average size is 2 to 5 kg but can attain a weight of 30 kilograms. Adults are easily identified by the largest pectoral fin of all tunas, extending well behind the commencement of the second dorsal fin. Juveniles have smaller pectoral fins but the distinctive white rear border of the tail fin differentiates albacore from juvenile yellowfin or bigeye tuna. Takes lures well and is excellent eating.

BONITO, AUSTRALIAN

Scientific name: *Sarda australis*. Also known as Bonny and occasionally horse mackerel.

Description: Commonly found in large schools on the coast of Victoria. Easily distinguished from other tunas and bonito species by the presence of narrow horizontal stripes on the lower part of the body. Bonito also have a single row of small but distinct conical teeth. The Australian bonito can grow to 1 m and nearly 8 kg but is usually less than 3 – 4 kilograms.

BARRACOUTA

Scientific name: *Thyrsites atun*. Also known as 'Couta, pickhandle, axehandle, occasionally by its South African name snoek.

Description: The barracouta is a member of the same family as gemfish (hake) which is a much deeper bodied fish. There is no resemblance to the more tropical barracuda.

The barracouta has a very long first dorsal with a distinctive black patch near the leading edge and around 5 finlets on the caudal peduncle (the gemfish has 2 finlets). The colour is steely grey and the small scales are easily shed. The barracouta has three large teeth on its upper jaw.

Grows to 4.5 kg and 1.3 m but commonly caught at 1 – 2 kilograms.

Fishing: Barracouta can take a variety of baits and lures. They are frequently taken on chrome spoons or casting lures. Barracouta will also take minnow lures and feathers and soft plastics, but their teeth make short work of all but the most robust lures.

A wire trace will help prevent bite offs of expensive lures and increase the catch rates with baits. Barracouta will take fish flesh, garfish or pilchard baits readily and while partial to live baits are difficult to hook due to a bony mouth and a habit of running with the bait across their jaws.

Barracouta should be handled carefully due to their sharp teeth which also have an anticoagulant which makes any cuts bleed profusely. Barracouta are considered good eating from Victorian waters.

Rigs & Tactics:

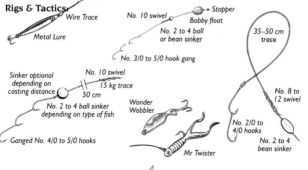

BREAM, BLACK

Scientific name: *Acanthopagrus butcheri*. Also known as Bream, blue nosed bream.

Description: The black bream is a very highly sought after angling species of the estuaries of the southern parts of Australia. The black bream looks very similar to the yellowfin bream and hybrids have been recorded from the Gippsland lakes in Victoria. The major difference is in fin colour, with the black bream possessing brownish or dusky ventral and anal fins. The mouth is fairly small with rows of peg like teeth and crushing plates on the palate. It reaches a maximum size of around 3.5 kg, but a specimen over 1 kg is highly regarded.

Fishing: This is one of the most sought after species in Australia. They are most commonly fished with a light line of 3 – 5 kilograms. Bait running reels on shorter rods are frequently used. Bream generally bite best on a rising tide and after dark but many quality fish, including on lures, are taken during the day and in ambush sites on the bottom half of the tide. Bream can be timid biters so as little weight as possible should be used and any sinker must run freely. Best baits are prawn and yabby, although beach, blood and squirt worms, pipi, anchovy or blue sardine and flesh baits also work extremely well. Some anglers make their own special dough baits out of flour and water with added meat, cheese, sugar, fish oils or other secret ingredients. When bream bite, it is important to let them run up to a metre before setting the hook. The bream will then run strongly for the nearest cover and many fish are lost on this initial surge. They are also excellent lure or soft plastic targets.

Rigs and Tactics:

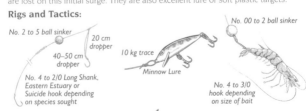

No. 2 to 5 ball sinker

20 cm dropper

40–50 cm dropper

No. 4 to 2/0 Long Shank, Eastern Estuary or Suicide hook depending on species sought

10 kg trace

Minnow Lure

No. 00 to 2 ball sinker

No. 4 to 3/0 hook depending on size of bait

BREAM, YELLOWFIN

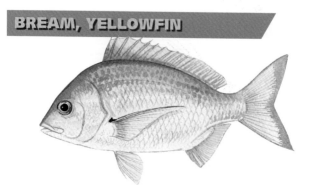

Scientific name: *Acanthopagrus australis*. Also known as Silver bream, sea bream, surf bream.

Description: The yellowfin bream is similar to other bream, but with a black spot at the base of the pectoral fin. Also has yellow or yellowish anal and ventral fins. Frequently taken from inshore oceanic waters where the colour is frequently silver, varying to dark olive from estuaries. Lacks the brown horizontal stripes and black stomach cavity lining of the similar tarwhine. Attains a maximum size of 66 cm and 4.4 kg but fish over a kilogram are noteworthy.

Fishing: Fantastic fishing for yellowfin bream can be had near the mouths of estuaries in winter when the fish moves downstream to spawn. Estuarine fish can be taken as described for black bream, with oyster leases, rock walls and edges of drop offs being prime spots. Berley works very well when fish are finicky. Yellowfin bream can be targeted with lightly weighted blue sardines, anchovies or half a pilchard cast into the edge of a good wash. When tailor or tommy rough are feeding, a bait which sinks through the tailor can take some thumping bream.

In the surf, pilchards which repeatedly come back with the gut area eaten out by small bites is a sign that bream may be present, especially if fishing the edges of gutters. A half a pilchard rigged on smaller hooks, a pipi or beach worm bait can take these fish. Bream are excellent lure and soft plastic targets.

Yellowfin bream are excellent eating although fish eating weed can have an iodine taint.

Rigs and Tactics:

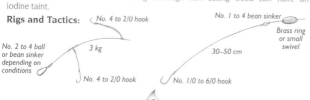

No. 4 to 2/0 hook

No. 2 to 4 ball or bean sinker depending on conditions

3 kg

No. 4 to 2/0 hook

No. 1 to 4 bean sinker

Brass ring or small swivel

30–50 cm

No. 1/0 to 6/0 hook

DORY, JOHN

Scientific name: *Zeus faber.* Also known as St Peter's fish, doorkeeper's fish, dory keparu (NZ).

Description: An unusual fish with a large, upward pointing mouth which can be extended the length of its head. The John dory has a distinctive, prominent mark on each side, said to be made by the fingers of St Peter when he picked up this fish. The John dory has very fine scales compared with the mirror dory which has no scales. The elongated dorsal rays give a distinctive appearance. John dory are most common near mid to deepwater reefs from 10 to 80 m but can be found in deeper estuaries.

The John dory can reach 75 cm and 4 kg although they are commonly taken at around a kilogram.

Fishing: The John dory is a poor fighter but it is absolutely delicious. The John dory is a common deep water trawl species in temperate waters but can be taken by anglers near deep reefs, wrecks and in deep estuaries such as the Hawkesbury. John dory greatly prefer live fish such as yellowtail for bait but can be caught on very fresh fillets.

Rigs and Tactics:

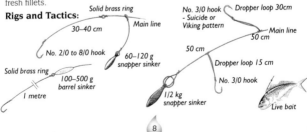

Solid brass ring
30–40 cm
Main line
No. 2/0 to 8/0 hook
60–120 g snapper sinker
Solid brass ring
100–500 g barrel sinker
I metre

No. 3/0 hook - Suicide or Viking pattern
Dropper loop 30cm
Main line
50 cm
50 cm
Dropper loop 15 cm
1/2 kg snapper sinker
No. 3/0 hook
Live bait

DRUMMER, SILVER

Scientific name: *Kyphosus sydneyanus*. Also known as Common buffalo bream, Sydney drummer.

Description: The silver drummer is a large schooling fish growing to 12 kg which offers better sport than eating. These mainly herbivorous fish are found in surge zones and near inshore reefs. They are dusky silver with fairly prominent lengthwise bands. The lips appear more prominent than in rock blackfish and the head is more pointed. The silver drummer can be separated from the similar western buffalo bream (*Kyphosus cornelii*) as the silver drummer has a black or uniformly dusky tail fin which is almost square and the dark, moustache-like line from the upper lip to the eye.

Fishing: Silver drummer are fished for with sea cabbage, bread, cunjevoi and prawns. Silver drummer are caught under floats in the surge zones or on lightly weighted baits fished near inshore reefs. Berley of bread, weed or cunjevoi works well.

Silver drummer fight hard but fair and make reasonable eating if bled and cleaned immediately, but larger specimens are definitely more fun to catch than to eat.

Rigs and Tactics:

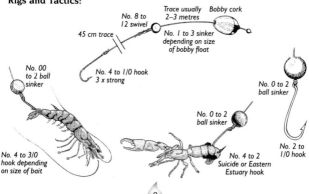

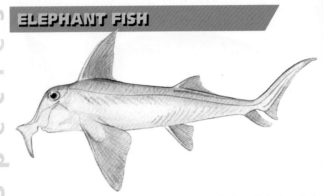

Scientific name: *Callorhynchus milii*. Also known as Elephant shark, ghost shark, whitefish, plownose chimera.

Description: The elephant fish is a unique species easily recognised by the fleshy nose which is used to find food in sandy or lightly silted bottoms. The pectoral fins are large and used like a ray for navigation. The eggs are spindle shaped, about 20 cm long and take 8 months to hatch.

Unlike most sharks, the elephant fish has a single gill slit. It has a prominent dorsal spine like a Port Jackson shark and can inflict a painful wound if not handled carefully.

Fishing: Until recently, these fish were shunned due to their ugly appearance. However, the flesh is white and firm and good eating and they are being increasingly targeted in southern bays and inlets in summer. Light bottom rigs get maximum sport from these fish. However it is important to realise that the summer fishery targets spawning fish and the take of these fish should be limited to ensure that they are not over-exploited.

Rigs and Tactics:

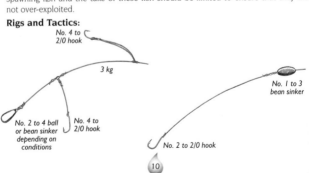

No. 4 to 2/0 hook

3 kg

No. 2 to 4 ball or bean sinker depending on conditions

No. 4 to 2/0 hook

No. 1 to 3 bean sinker

No. 2 to 2/0 hook

FLATHEAD, DUSKY

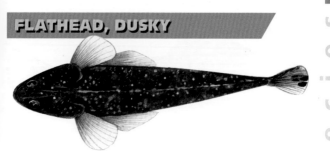

Scientific name: Platycephalus fuscus. Also known as Estuary flathead, mud flathead, black flathead, flattie, frog and lizard (especially large specimens).

Description: The dusky flathead is the largest of the 30 species of flathead in Australia, reaching 10 kg and 150 centimetres. Any fish above 5 kg is certainly worth boasting about. The flathead shape is unmistakable, and the dusky flathead also has the sharp opercular (cheek) spines to spike the unwary. The colouration is highly variable from light fawn to black depending on the type of bottom they are found on. The belly ranges from creamy yellow to white.

The tail fin features a characteristic dark spot in the top end corner and a patch of blue on the lower half. This is an estuarine or inshore species. This feature plus its large size and good eating make it the ultimate prize for many weekend anglers.

Rig and Tactics:

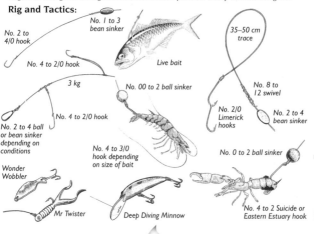

No. 2 to 4/0 hook

No. 1 to 3 bean sinker

Live bait

No. 4 to 2/0 hook

3 kg

No. 4 to 2/0 hook

No. 2 to 4 ball or bean sinker depending on conditions

No. 00 to 2 ball sinker

No. 4 to 3/0 hook depending on size of bait

35–50 cm trace

No. 8 to 12 swivel

No. 2/0 Limerick hooks

No. 2 to 4 bean sinker

No. 0 to 2 ball sinker

Wonder Wobbler

Mr Twister

Deep Diving Minnow

No. 4 to 2 Suicide or Eastern Estuary hook

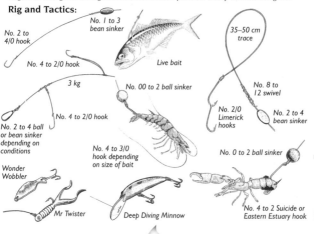

Saltwater Species

FLATHEAD, EASTERN BLUE SPOT

Scientific name: *Platycephalus caeruleopuntatus*. Also known as Blue-spotted flathead, drift flathead, longnose flathead, red spotted flathead.

Description: Flathead identification can be quite difficult, but the Eastern blue spot flathead has three or four black ovals or bars on the lower part of the tail fin. This species is generally found at a length of less than 45 centimetres. The eastern blue spot flathead is a common catch on the sand banks of NSW.

FLATHEAD, SAND

Scientific name: *Platycephalus arenarius* (Northern sand flathead), *Platycephalus bassensis* (Southern sand flathead). Also known as Northern-flag tailed flathead; Southern - slimy flathead, bay flathead, common flathead, sandy flathead.

Description: The various sand flatheads are generally smaller than the blue-spotted or dusky flathead. The northern sand flathead can reach 45 cm but is more commonly encountered in large numbers at around 30 cm in estuaries or on adjacent beaches. They can be found to a depth of 30 fathoms. They have a distinctive pattern of long, horizontal black stripes on its tail. The southern sand flathead has two or sometimes three squared off black patches on the lower part of the tail fin. This species is reputed to reach over 3 kg but is rarely found over a kilogram.

saltwater Species

FLATHEAD, TIGER

Scientific name: *Neoplatycephalus richardsoni.* Also known as Trawl flathead, king flathead, spiky flathead, toothy flathead.

Description: Tiger flathead have a somewhat more cylindrical body compared to the obviously compressed form of the other flathead. Tiger flathead colour varies but generally has a reddish-orange or reddish-brown base colour but with brighter orange spots which extend to the tail. The tiger flathead has large teeth on the roof of the mouth. The maximum size is 2.5 kg but they are most often encountered from 0.5 to 1.5 kilograms.

Fishing: Tiger flathead are a common trawl species in the south-eastern waters to a depth of 80 fathoms. However, in parts of Victoria and Tasmania they can enter bays, harbours and estuaries. As they are often taken from deep water, heavy handlines or boat rods and typical paternoster rigs with up to four droppers are used. Baits of fish flesh, pilchards, squid or prawns take most fish. In shallower water, live baits prove deadly. Tiger flathead are a highly regarded food fish.

Rigs and Tactics:

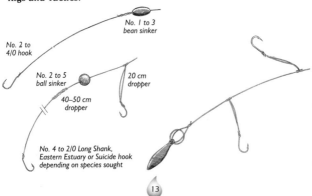

No. 1 to 3 bean sinker

No. 2 to 4/0 hook

No. 2 to 5 ball sinker

20 cm dropper

40–50 cm dropper

No. 4 to 2/0 Long Shank, Eastern Estuary or Suicide hook depending on species sought

FLATHEAD, YANK

Scientific name: *Platycephalus speculator*. Also known as Southern Blue-Spotted flathead, yank flathead, Southern flathead, Castelnau's flathead, southern dusky flathead, bluespot flathead, long nose flathead, shovelnose flathead.

Description: This flathead can be distinguished on the basis of grey-green spots on the top half of the tail and 3 to 5 large black spots on the lower portion, surrounded by white or off-white. This species also has only one dorsal spine compared with two for many other flathead. The yank or southern blue-spotted flathead, can reach a maximum size of nearly 8 kg, although any fish of 3 kg is rare and it is much more common at around a kilogram.

Fishing: The yank flathead can be found in similar areas to other flatheads, ambushing prey wherever possible. This species can occasionally be found over weed patches or around the edges of weeds. It is not as commonly taken on lures and can be a welcome bonus when fishing for King George whiting or when baits sink through berley fishing for herring and garfish. Like all the flathead, the southern blue-spotted is good eating.

Rigs and Tactics:

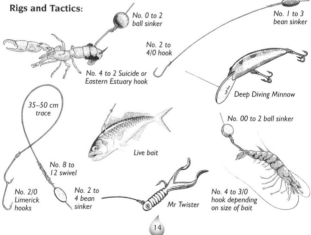

No. 0 to 2 ball sinker

No. 1 to 3 bean sinker

No. 2 to 4/0 hook

No. 4 to 2 Suicide or Eastern Estuary hook

Deep Diving Minnow

35–50 cm trace

No. 00 to 2 ball sinker

Live bait

No. 8 to 12 swivel

No. 2/0 Limerick hooks

No. 2 to 4 bean sinker

Mr Twister

No. 4 to 3/0 hook depending on size of bait

FLOUNDER, GREENBACK

Scientific name: *Pseudorhombus arsius*. Also known as Flounder.

Description: The large toothed flounder is a left eyed flounder, i.e. both eyes are on the left side after the right eye migrates around the head during juvenile development. This species has highly variable colouration which can change rapidly, depending on the bottom where it is found. It ranges from the shallow mud and sand banks of estuaries to depths of 35 fathoms. The large toothed flounder possesses large front teeth in its upper and lower jaws. Reaches 50 cm and more than 1 kg but is most common at 30 to 35 centimetres. Flounders have a separate tail which easily distinguishes them from the sole which is another flat fish.

FLOUNDER, LARGE TOOTHED

Scientific name: *Pseudorhombus arsius*. Also known as Flounder.

Description: The large toothed flounder is a left eyed flounder, i.e. both eyes are on the left side after the right eye migrates around the head during juvenile development. This species has highly variable colouration which can change rapidly, depending on the bottom where it is found. It ranges from the shallow mud and sand banks of estuaries to depths of 35 fathoms. The large toothed flounder possesses large front teeth in its upper and lower jaws. Reaches 50 cm and more than 1 kg but is most common at 30 to 35 centimetres. Flounders have a separate tail which easily distinguishes them from the sole which is another flat fish.

GARFISH, RIVER

Scientific name: *Hyporhamphus regularis.* Also known as Gardie, beakie, needle gar, splinter gar, lakes garfish.

Description: The river garfish is similar in appearance to the sea garfish, but the body is slightly more stout and the silver stripe is not so prominent. The river gar also has quite large scales which are obvious when they become dislodged with handling. The beak is generally dull coloured except for the red or orange tip. The upper jaw is broader than it is long. River garfish reach 35 centimetres.

Fishing: Maggots are a particularly favoured bait in many areas. River gar are not as highly regarded as food as sea gar and need to be scaled before consumption. They are a fantastic bait for tailor, mulloway and other pelagic species.

GARFISH, SOUTHERN SEA

Scientific name: *Hyporhamphus melanochir.* Also known as South Australian garfish.

Description: An attractive slender fish with fine delicate scales. This species is more common in estuaries or near shore seagrass areas. The southern sea garfish reaches 50 cm and the anal fin starts below the front of the dorsal fin. The silver stripe on the side is particularly prominent.

Fishing: A common and enjoyable species to catch over or adjacent to seagrass meadows where mixed bags of Tommy rough, King George whiting and squid can be taken from the same pollard and pilchard oil berley trail. The southern sea garfish makes excellent eating.

GRENADIER

Scientific name: *Macruronus novaezelandiae*. Also known as Blue hake, blue grenadier, whiptail, hoki.

Description: The grenadier is a long bronze-blue fish with a distinct lateral line, the second dorsal fin is low and reaches to the end of the tapered tail where it joins the also extended anal fin. Fins are purplish-blue. Commonly found in depths of 20 to 60 m, juveniles occur in southern bays and estuaries up to tidal influences. Adults reach 1.1 metres.

Fishing: The grenadier is a common trawl species, especially in New Zealand where it is marketed as hoki fillets. The flesh is firm but is not as highly valued as many other species. Grenadier are taken while fishing for other species using standard bottom paternoster rigs. Grenadier readily take fish baits, squid and prawns. As with many deeper species, their fight is affected by the depth and heavier lines and sinkers commonly used.

GURNARD, RED

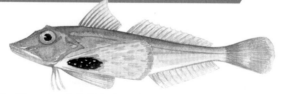

Scientific name: *Chelidonichthys kumu*. Also known as Gurnard, flying gurnard, latchet, kumu gurnard, kumukumu.

Description: The red gurnard is a beautiful species with its large pectoral fins and brightly patterned ventral fins which are bright blue with a large black spot and scattered paler spots. The first three rays of the pectoral fin are free and act as 'fingers' for the detection of food in the sand. While the head is bony, it is smooth and the red gurnard lacks the bony horns of some other species.

The red gurnard can reach 60 cm and more than 2 kg but is more common at 40 – 45 centimetres.

It is commonly found from 80 m to the continental shelf but can be taken from shallower waters at times.

GROPER, EASTERN BLUE

Scientific name: *Achoerodus viridis* (Eastern blue groper).

Also known as Red groper, brown groper (Actually female colouration of the Eastern blue groper), giant pigfish, blue tank.

Description: The eastern blue groper can reach 20 kg but has been seriously over fished in many areas and fish of 2 to 10 kg are much more likely. The blue gropers are easily identified by their size, often brilliant colours, their fleshy lips, heavy scales and peg like teeth.

Eastern blue groper prefer turbulent rocky shorelines or inshore bomboras. This species is protected from spearfishing.

Fishing: Blue groper present a real test for shore based anglers. They can be taken on cunjevoi, prawns and squid, fresh crabs, and especially the red crabs found in the intertidal areas of the east coast. Crabs are easily the best bait. Heavy rods and line and extra strong hooks are required for these hard, dirty fighters. A groper should not be given its head as it will bury you in the nearest cave or under any rock ledge. Small to medium blue groper are good eating, but large ones are dry and the flesh coarse. These are hardy fish which many anglers choose to return to the water, as their fight is their best and most memorable feature.

Rigs and Tactics:

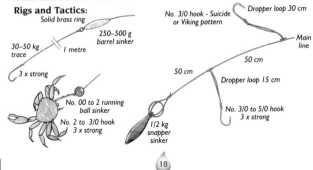

Solid brass ring

30–50 kg trace
1 metre

250–500 g barrel sinker

3 x strong

No. 00 to 2 running ball sinker

No. 2 to 3/0 hook 3 x strong

No. 3/0 hook - Suicide or Viking pattern

Dropper loop 30 cm

Main line

50 cm

Dropper loop 15 cm

50 cm

1/2 kg snapper sinker

No. 3/0 to 5/0 hook 3 x strong

HERRING, AUSTRALIAN

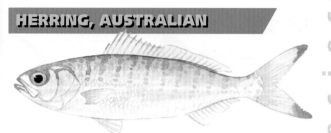

Scientific name: *Arripis georgiana*. Also known as Tommy rough, tommy, ruff, bull herring, Western herring.

Description: A pretty and highly sought after species, the Australian herring is not a 'true' hering from the family Clupidae. Although the Australian herring can reach 40 cm, they are commonly caught at between 22 and 28 centimetres. The herring is similar to a juvenile Australian salmon, but the herring has a larger eye, black tips on the ends of the tail fin lobes and no black blotch at the base of the pectoral fin. The herring's scales feel rough when rubbed towards the head whereas an Australian salmon feels smooth which gives rise to the common name 'ruff'.

Fishing: Australian herring specialists can turn angling for these scrappy little fighters in to an art form. Standard rigs include a wooden blob (float) whose hole is filled with pollard and pilchard oil, a reasonably long trace and a bait of maggot, prawn, squid or blue bait. When biting freely, Australian herring are taken on pieces of green drinking straw as bait.

Herring are an inshore schooling fish which is commonly taken from rock groynes and beaches and are attracted to berley slicks when boat angling, especially inshore around shallow sea grass beds. Best berley includes bread, pollard, finely chopped fish scraps and chip pieces leftover from the local fish and chip shop. Herring are also taken on lures, with Halco wobblers and Tassie Devils or any small lure with red working well. On lures, herring jump as well as their cousins the salmon and although some throw the hooks, they are terrific fun. Herring are also very good eating and far superior to Australian salmon.

Rigs and Tactics:

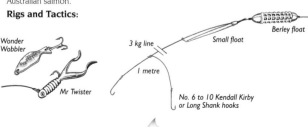

Wonder Wobbler

Mr Twister

3 kg line

1 metre

Small float

Berley float

No. 6 to 10 Kendall Kirby or Long Shank hooks

KINGFISH, YELLOWTAIL

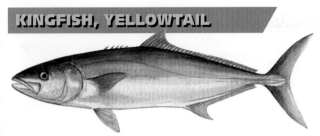

Scientific name: *Seriola lalandi*. Also known as Kingie, yellowtail, hoodlum and bandit.

Description: The yellowtail kingfish is a beautiful, powerful fish which has a large, deeply forked tail. The back and upper sides are dark, purply blue while the lower part of the body is white. These two distinctive colours are separated by a yellow band which varies in width and intensity from fish to fish. The tail is a bright yellow. This can be a large fish reaching 2 m and more than 50 kg although increasing commercial and recreational fishing is affecting the presence of large fish. Any yellowtail kingfish over 20 kg will be a memorable capture.

Fishing: The yellowtail kingfish is a brutal, dirty fighter which will fully test the skill of the angler and the quality of their gear. The first run of a kingfish is straight towards the nearest bottom obstruction to cut off an unwary angler. Kingfish will take a wide variety of lures such as minnow lures, soft plastics and flies. Vertical jigging with metal lures can be deadly at times. They will take a range of whole and cut fish baits, prawns, squid, octopus and cuttlefish but there are occasions when they can be finicky. At other times yellowtail kingfish will strike at bare hooks. Live bait is almost certain to attract a mad rush from any kingfish in the area.

Kingfish were previously considered average eating, but they have been increasingly recognised as a quality fish, including as sashimi. Large fish are worse eating and can have worms in the flesh.

Rigs and Tactics:

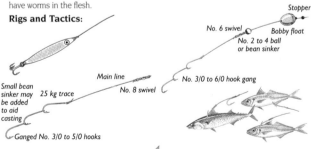

LEATHERJACKET, ROUGH

Scientific name: *Scobinichthys granulatus*.

Description: This species reaches 34 cm and has no notch for the prominent dorsal spine to lay back into. The rough leather jacket has a large ventral flap, three dark lines across the forehead and dark blotchings over the back and sides. It is common in coastal seagrass beds and adjacent reefs and in estuaries.

Fishing: The rough leatherjacket will take prawns, squid, crabs, worms and cut baits. A wire trace or long shank hook can prevent bite-offs. A light line and minimal weight for the conditions can improve the fight of leatherjackets. This species is good eating.

LING, ROCK

Scientific name: *Genypterus tigerinus*. Also known as Tiger ling.

Description: The body of the rock ling is pale grey to white and densely patterned in black.

The dorsal and anal fins lack black bars which are found on the similar pink ling. The 'beard' is actually a modified ventral fin which is positioned under the chin. Easily separated from the beardie as the rock ling does not have a tail and the dorsal and anal fins meet at the end of the body. This species can be found to depths of 60 m and adults are found on rocky reefs and broken ground while juveniles are found inshore and in bays and estuaries.

Fishing: Taken as part of mixed reef catches in cooler waters with standard reef paternoster rigs. The rock ling prefers fresh baits of cut and whole fish, squid and cuttlefish baits. This is an excellent food fish and a welcome bonus in a mixed bag.

LEATHERJACKET, SIX SPINED

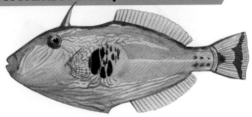

Scientific name: *Meuschenia freycineti*. Also known as variable leatherjacket.

Description: The six-spined leatherjacket can reach the respectable size of 60 cm, with larger specimens found from the south coast population, although the east coast fish can be more brightly coloured. The six-spined leatherjacket is most easily identified by the prominent scribble pattern in blue or brown on the head and front part of the body. The dorsal and anal fins are yellow in the adult. The tail fin often has a black blotch at its base and a prominent black stripe, especially males. Males often have a yellow and brown blotch on their sides. Females are much less brightly coloured. There are 5 to 8 spines on each side of the wrist of the tail.

Adults are usually encountered on coastal reefs whereas juveniles, which often have prominent brown stripes along the sides and less prominent scribbling on the head, are common on seagrass meadows of estuaries and coastal bays.

Fishing: Like all leatherjackets, the six-spined leatherjacket has a small mouth and a capacity to pick larger baits intended for the larger reef fish. They show a marked preference for squid or prawn baits but can be taken on a wide variety of baits. A fairly small, long shanked hook is recommended and some anglers use a light wire trace to avoid bite-offs. The difficulty in hooking leatherjackets is more than offset by their excellent eating qualities. They can be headed and the skin peeled off by hand for a very high quality meal.

Rigs and Tactics:

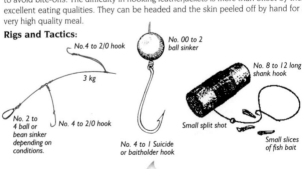

No. 4 to 2/0 hook

3 kg

No. 2 to 4 ball or bean sinker depending on conditions.

No. 4 to 2/0 hook

No. 00 to 2 ball sinker

No. 4 to 1 Suicide or baitholder hook

No. 8 to 12 long shank hook

Small split shot

Small slices of fish bait

LUDERICK

Scientific name: *Girella tricuspidata*. Also known as Blackfish, darkie, bronzie.

Description: The luderick has up to 12 narrow vertical dark bars on its upper body. The colour varies from almost black to a pale purplish colour depending on the wash in the area of capture. The tail fin is darker than the body.

Luderick are a schooling species, although the largest specimens form much smaller groups. Luderick can reach more than 2 kg but are more common at 500-900 grams. Fishing for this species is less popular than in NSW where it is highly prized.

MACKEREL, FRIGATE

Scientific name: *Auxis thazard*. Also known as Little tuna.

Description: A handsome fish which can reach 60 cm and around 5 kilograms. The frigate mackerel possesses the distinctive broken oblique lines above the lateral line and no markings below the lateral line. It can be easily separated from the similar mackerel tuna as the frigate mackerel has a wide gap between the two dorsal fins, no black spots near the ventral fins and a more slender body. The frigate mackerel can form large shoals in coastal or inshore waters.

MACKEREL, SLIMY

Scientific name: *Scomber australasicus*. Also known as Blue mackerel, spotted chub mackerel, slimies.

Description: A relatively small species, reaching 65 cm and 2 kg but which is most often encountered at 25 – 35 centimetres. The slimy mackerel has wavy bars on its back, spots on its side and 5 – 6 finlets behind both the dorsal and anal fins. It can be separated from the jack or horse mackerel as it lacks the bony scutes along the rear of the lateral line. Slimy mackerel travel in schools which can enter bays and some larger estuaries. The slimy mackerel is an extremely important forage species with many pelagic species attracted to feed on slimies. The decimation of pilchard stocks by virus has made slimies even more important. Proposals to increase commercial slimy mackerel exploitation has angered recreational fishers as the impact on local fishing quality is likely to be severe.

MARLIN, BLACK

Scientific name: *Makaira indica*. Also known as Giant black marlin, silver marlin.

Description: A magnificent blue water billfish capable of reaching a length of nearly 5 m and 850 kilograms. The black marlin is readily distinguished by its rigid pectoral fins which cannot be laid next to body in any black marlin and are completely rigid in all fish over 50 kg. In this fairly heavy bodied fish, the start of the second dorsal is forward to the start of the second anal fin. Black marlin are most commonly found in blue water, with fish moving southwards as far as Victoria with the warmer currents. Black marlin are found near current lines and where baitfish aggregations are prevalent.

MORWONG

Scientific name: Nemadactylus douglasii. Also known as Grey morwong, silver morwong, blue morwong, common morwong, rubberlip, blubberlip, jackass, mowie, sea bream, porae (New Zealand).

Description: The morwong is a deep bodied fish with a relatively small mouth and prominent fleshy lips. The colour ranges from a pale grey to silver and to silvery blue. In common with other morwong, this species has several extended rays in each pectoral fin. Morwong can reach 70 cm and more than 4 kg, but is commonly caught at 1 – 2 kilograms. The morwong can be separated from the banded morwong and red morwong by their distinctive colourations and the queen snapper has distinctive gold lines on the head in large adults and gold stripes on smaller fish.

Fishing: The morwong was once considered a poor second alternative to snapper, particularly in NSW, but increasingly scarce snapper numbers have elevated morwong as a more desirable species.

Morwong feed on prawns, worms, squid, molluscs, fish flesh and other food which they encounter opportunistically. Best baits include fish flesh, prawns, squid and octopus tentacles. Baits are best presented on a traditional two hook paternoster rig, with sufficient weight to reach the bottom and bounce along the bottom on a slow drift. Morwong are often found in small loose schools so once fish are encountered, repeated drifts over the same area should continue to produce fish. If the current or wind is strong, a drogue or drift anchor will slow the drift and keep the baits in productive water which includes the edges of deep water reefs and drop-offs, with broken rock and gravel being particularly important. On occasions morwong can be taken over sand or mud bottoms, but a depth sounder is important to save time as fish feed more infrequently in these areas.

Morwong are most commonly encountered from 30 to 200 m, but they are occasionally taken from shallower waters. They are an easy target for spearfishermen. The morwong is fair to good eating but can have a slight iodine taste, especially if fish have been grazing on weed which they occasionally do. Filleting helps improve the quality of the flesh.

Rigs and Tactics:

MULLET, SAND

Scientific name: *Myxus elongatus*. Also known as Tallegalane, black spot mullet, lano.

Description: The sand mullet is a moderately small mullet reaching 41 cm and nudging a kilogram but most commonly encountered around 25 – 30 centimetres.

This species has a straight upper profile and pointed head which differs from the sea mullet which has a more rounded snout. The sand mullet generally has a black blotch at the top of the base of the pectoral fin. The sand mullet lacks the obvious fatty eyelid of the sea mullet and several other species. The eye colour is yellow-brown or light brown as opposed to the bright yellow of the yellow-eye mullet, but the most obvious difference is that the sand mullet has 9 rays in the anal fin and the yellow-eye mullet 12 rays. The sand mullet is found in bays, lower estuaries and ocean beaches in schools, usually of similar sized fish. They have a strong preference for sandy bottoms but can be found over mud or weed bottoms on occasions.

MULLET, SEA

Scientific name: *Mugil cephalus*. Also known as Bully mullet, bully, mullet, hard-gut mullet, river mullet. Juveniles referred to as poddy mullet or poddies.

Description: The sea mullet is a cylindrical barrel of muscle which is readily identified by the thick, transparent, gelatinous covering over all but the centre of the eyes. They often have several diffuse lateral stripes on the side, but the colour and intensity can vary with the environment. Sea mullet have a distinguishing enlarged and pointed scale behind the top of the pectoral fin.

Sea mullet are found from far above the tidal reaches of coastal rivers to reasonable distances offshore, but they are best known for the vast shoals they can form at spawning time on east coast beaches. They are a very large species, reaching 80 cm and over 5 kg, but sea mullet are most commonly encountered at 1 – 2 kilograms.

MULLOWAY

Scientific name: *Argyrosomus japonicus*. Also known as Jewfish, jew, jewie, butterfish, river kingfish, silver kingfish.

Small fish to around 3 kg are generally referred to as soapies due to their rather bland or soapy taste. Fish from 3 – 8 kg are frequently known as Schoolies as they are often encountered in schools which decrease in number as the size increases.

Description: Mulloway are a large and highly prized species found in estuaries, embayments and inshore ocean waters throughout its range. The mulloway can vary in colour from dark bronze to silver and there may be red or purple tinges, but a silver ocean mulloway is a stunning fish.

The mulloway has large scales and a generous mouth. A line of silvery spots follows the lateral line in live fish which glows under artificial lights as do the eyes which shine a bright red. A conspicuous black spot is just above the pectoral fin.

The tail fin is convex (rounded outwards) and this characteristic differentiates them from the smaller teraglin which has a concave tail and a yellow inside of the mouth.

Mulloway can reach 1.8 m and more than 60 kg, but any fish over 25 kg is worth long term boasting rights for the angler. Mulloway are most commonly caught at 3 – 10 kilograms.

Rigs and Tactics:

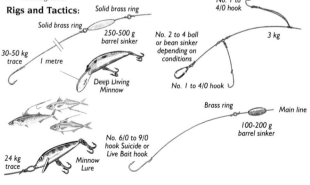

Solid brass ring

Solid brass ring

250-500 g barrel sinker

30-50 kg trace   I metre

Deep Diving Minnow

No. I to 4/0 hook

3 kg

No. 2 to 4 ball or bean sinker depending on conditions

No. I to 4/0 hook

24 kg trace

Minnow Lure

No. 6/0 to 9/0 hook Suicide or Live Bait hook

Brass ring

Main line

100-200 g barrel sinker

NANNYGAI

Scientific name: *Centroberyx affinis*. Also known as Eastern nannygai, redfish.

Description: A pink to bright red or orange coloured fish, with large eyes, a large upturned mouth, a rounded snout and no pale fin margins. The nannygai is separated from other similar species such as the red snapper as it has 7 as opposed to 6 dorsal spines. While juveniles can school in estuaries and on inshore reefs, larger fish are found in larger schools in waters deeper than 25 m and out towards the edge of the continental shelf where they are a common trawl species. The nannygai is not a large fish, reaching around 45 centimetres.

Fishing: The nannygai is often encountered when fishing deeper reefs for snapper and other deep water species. The large weights and relatively small size of nannygai means that they are less highly regarded than many other species. The large mouth and schooling nature of the nannygai means that large numbers can be caught, and on large baits.

Standard snapper paternoster rigs with sufficient weight to drag bottom on a drift will take nannygai. Nannygai can be found near offshore reefs or near drop-offs over gravel or silt bottoms. Nannygai will take baits of fish, squid, octopus, crab, prawn and pilchard. When nannygai are biting freely, a fish can be caught on each hook on each drop and will often beat any snapper or other target species to the hook. Nannygai make good eating with firm white fillets. They are taken by trawlers in large quantities which are marketed as redfish.

Rigs and Tactics:

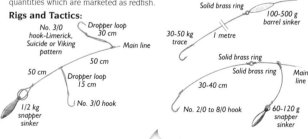

No. 3/0 hook-Limerick, Suicide or Viking pattern

Dropper loop 30 cm

Main line

50 cm

50 cm

Dropper loop 15 cm

No. 3/0 hook

1/2 kg snapper sinker

Solid brass ring

100-500 g barrel sinker

30-50 kg trace

1 metre

Solid brass ring

Solid brass ring

Main line

30-40 cm

No. 2/0 to 8/0 hook

60-120 g snapper sinker

PERCH, ESTUARY

Scientific name: *Macquaria colonorum*. Also known as Perch.

Description: The estuary perch is easily confused with Australian bass which can be found in the same areas. Even experienced anglers have difficulty telling the two species apart. The most obvious distinguishing feature is the head profile which is indented or concave in estuary perch and rounded in bass. Estuary perch are very rarely found above the tidal influence of rivers. Estuary perch are also increasingly common in southern waters. Like bass, larger specimens are all female and they must have access to salt water to breed.

Fishing: Estuary perch are an excellent fighting and eating fish, but like their cousin the bass, most are returned unhurt today. They are aggressive and can be over-fished by skilled fishers. Estuary perch take surface and deep diving lures and larger flies well, fishing very close to snags and bank-side cover in tidal areas. Accurate casts, within 30 cm of the snag and patience at the beginning of the retrieve gets the best results. Estuary perch are also caught with bait in deep holes in lower tidal reaches during winter spawning aggregations. Estuary perch are particularly partial to a live prawn fished under a float near snags or drop-offs near cumbungi beds. Other popular baits, fished under a float or with minimal weight include live fish, crickets, worms and crabs.

Rigs and Tactics:

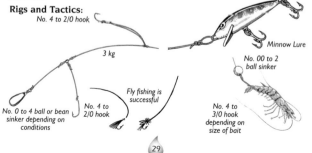

No. 4 to 2/0 hook

3 kg

Minnow Lure

No. 00 to 2 ball sinker

Fly fishing is successful

No. 0 to 4 ball or bean sinker depending on conditions

No. 4 to 2/0 hook

No. 4 to 3/0 hook depending on size of bait

saltwater species

PERCH, MAGPIE

Scientific name: *Cheilodactylus nigripes*. Also known as magpie morwong, black-striped morwong.

Description: A distinctive species with a white overall colour with broad black and grey bands. The mouth is quite small and like most morwongs the pectoral fin is large and may be coloured. This species is separated from the similar crested morwong (Cheilodactylus gibbosus) by range as the crested morwong is found from Newcastle to Bundaberg in Queensland and the first dorsal spine is obviously elongated while the fourth dorsal spine is longest in the magpie perch.

The magpie perch is generally a shallow water reef dweller, although juveniles are found in deeper estuaries. This species prefers reef and weed margins and will venture onto sand to feed. The magpie perch reaches 40 cm and 2 kilograms.

PIKE, LONGFINNED

Scientific name: *Dinolestes lewini*. Also known as Pike, jack pike, skipjack pike.

Description: The longfinned pike is a long slender fish with a large head, large mouth and an underslung jaw extending almost to the front edge of the large eye. This species has two distinct dorsal fins. A prominent and extended anal fin separates this species from the similar striped seapike which also has 2 – 3 brown lateral stripes along its side. The tail and wrist of the tail of the long finned pike are yellow or golden whereas in the striped seapike the tail has a yellow hue, especially near the back edge. The longfinned pike can be confused with the snook, which has the two dorsal fins widely separated and the ventral fin is set well behind the pectoral fin. The snook is a much larger species, reaching more than a metre and over 5 kilograms.

The longfinned pike can reach more than 2 kg and 90 cm but is most often encountered at between 40 and 50 centimetres.

RAY, EAGLE

Scientific name: *Aetobatus narinari*. Also known as Spotted eagle ray, duckbill ray, flying ray, white-spotted eagle ray.

Description: The eagle ray has a shining brown-black top of the body with a large number of white spots on the back half of the body. The eagle ray has an unusual bulging head with a long and tapering snout which is flattened rather like a duck's bill. The teeth are shaped like a chevron and are used for crushing oysters, pipis and other molluscs.

The tail is very long and thin and is around 4 times the width of the body. The eagle ray has 2 – 6 barbed spines at the base of the tail. The eagle ray is a very large species, reaching a width of around 3.5 m, but it is commonly seen at around 1.8 metres.

RAY, FIDDLER

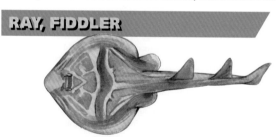

Scientific name: *Trygonorhina fasciata*. Also known as magpie ray, southern fiddler ray.

Description: A beautifully marked species, the fiddler ray is actually rarely taken by line fishermen but is often seen in shallow sandy bays throughout its range and can be part of the by-catch of prawn trawlers. The fiddler ray has a brown body covered in a pattern of blue bars often edged in black.

The fiddler ray grows to 1.2 m and has a round head region, small flaps and a long tail region.

The head shape differs from the shovelnose rays which have a triangular head shape.

saltwater Species

SALMON, AUSTRALIAN

Scientific name: *Arripis trutta* (Eastern species). Also known as Salmon, black back, cocky salmon, colonial salmon, kahawai. Salmon trout and bay trout, (juveniles).

Description: These 'salmon' species are not related to true trout and salmon in the family Salmonidae and are more closely related to the mullets. Australian salmon species reaches 7 kg.

The forked tail of adult salmon is dark, and the eye is generally yellow. The body is classically torpedo shaped and full of power. The head is quite large, and the mouth moderately large. There are distinctive brown dots or dashes along the dorsal surface although the larger specimens become dark across the back. The belly is silvery to white. The Australian salmon moves up the east coast in large schools on a northern spawning migration.

Fishing: The Australian salmon is one of the best light tackle sportsfish in Australia. They are the best fighting fish taken from the beach, where their strong runs and spectacular leaps more than compensate for the average eating quality.

Australian salmon form large schools as they move around the coasts, making them vulnerable to commercial fishing. There is little doubt that commercial fishing can affect local abundance and recreational fishing quality. These schools can provide spectacular fishing, but on occasions these schooling fish will not feed. Australian salmon are frequently caught on pilchards and cut baits, with belly fillets or baits with white skin attached doing better. Pipis, cockles and beach worms take many fish and can really surprise an unsuspecting whiting fisherman. In estuaries, salmon trout are often taken on whitebait, blue bait, prawns or squid. When Australian salmon are heavily fished, live bait will entice a strike when the freshest baits fail. The bite of the salmon is frequently quite fumbling and some patience is required before setting the hook.

Rigs and Tactics:

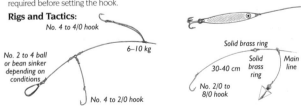

No. 4 to 4/0 hook

6–10 kg

No. 2 to 4 ball or bean sinker depending on conditions

No. 4 to 2/0 hook

Solid brass ring

Solid brass ring

Main line

30-40 cm

No. 2/0 to 8/0 hook

SERGEANT BAKER

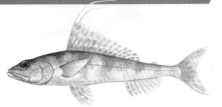

Scientific name: *Aulopus purpurissatus*.

Description: A reasonably common fish of deeper coastal reefs and adjacent sandy patches, but can move into larger bays on occasion. Sergeant baker have a red, ruddy or rusty brown colour and a small adipose-like second dorsal fin. The longer first dorsal fin unusually does not have any spines, only soft rays and the second and third ray is elongated in male fish.

The caudal fin is forked and the pectoral fins are large but the sergeant baker lacks the distinctive 'fingers' or bony head ridges of the gurnards. The sergeant baker reaches 70 cm in length and around 3 kg, but is more common at around 45 to 50 centimetres. It is average eating.

SHARK, BRONZE WHALER

Scientific name: *Carcharhinus brachyurus*. Also known as Copper shark, cocktail shark.

Description: A fairly common shark of offshore waters, but which occasionally enters large embayments. The bronze whaler is dangerous and has been responsible for several fatalities in Australia.

The bronze whaler is very similar to the black or whaler shark but the bronze whaler generally has a bronze or coppery colour, which fades to grey after death. The upper teeth are narrow and slightly concave on this species. The bronze whaler lacks the distinctive skin ridge running between the two dorsal fins which is present on the black whaler. The bronze whaler reaches 3.25 m and more than 200 kilograms.

Scientific name: *Mustelus antarcticus*. Also known as Sweet William.

Description: The gummy shark is a small, harmless shark reaching only 1.75 metres. The teeth in both jaws are smooth and flattened and arranged in a flat pavement-like pattern. The gummy shark looks similar to the school shark, but the school shark's teeth are sharp and triangular and the tail fin has a broad and deeply notched upper lobe, giving a double tail appearance.

The upper body of the gummy shark is covered with small white spots which are less apparent in larger fish.

Fishing: The gummy shark is frequently taken by anglers on deeper water snapper grounds with standard snapper baits and rigs. The gummy shark is more common on deeper water grounds and is a commercial fishing target which has been seriously overfished in many southern waters. The gummy shark can move into shallow water on occasion.

The best baits for gummy shark are squid, cuttlefish, octopus, pilchard and any fresh fish baits.

They are most often taken on the bottom hook of a snapper paternoster rig.

The gummy shark makes excellent eating and is highly regarded.

Rigs and Tactics:

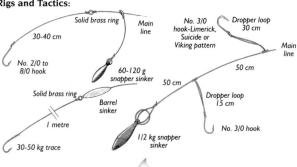

SHARK, MAKO

Scientific name: Isurus oxyrinchus. Also known as Shortfin mako, blue pointer, jumping shark.

Description: The mako shark is a sleek, beautifully streamlined close relative of the great white. The mako differs from the great white in being more streamlined and having distinctly pointed and hooked upper teeth as opposed to the distinctly triangular teeth in the great white. The mako is distinctly blue in colour though this fades to grey-blue after death. The pectoral fin is shorter than in the blue shark. The mako prefers deep offshore waters, but can move into more coastal waters where its sleek form and hooked teeth make short work of any hooked fish. If the hooked fish is skull dragged past the mako, it can provoke an attack on the boat, leaving teeth in the hull and very shaken fishermen. The mako is the most prized shark for game fishing, but is extremely dangerous for small boat fishermen.

SHARK, PORT JACKSON

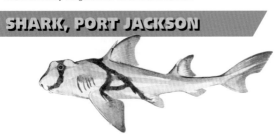

Scientific name: Heterodontus portusjacksoni. Also known as Bull shark, horn shark.

Description: The Port Jackson shark is a harmless species of inshore reefs and adjacent sand and weed patches which may group together in large numbers. The Port Jackson shark is an extremely primitive species readily identifiable by the bony ridge above the eye and a strong dorsal spine in front of both dorsal fins. The teeth are small and pointed in the front of the jaws with crushing teeth to the rear.

The Port Jackson shark lays the distinctive 'Mermaid's purse' egg case which is attached to kelp and is frequently washed up on beaches after storms. The Port Jackson shark can reach 2 m but is more common at around a metre.

SHARK, SCHOOL

Scientific name: Galeorhinus galeus. Also known as Snapper shark, eastern school shark, greyboy, grey shark, soupfin shark, tope.

Description: The school shark is a very slow growing, small and harmless species which is common in cool southern waters. It is more common in offshore areas, where it forms the basis of a substantial, but overfished commercial fishery. Juveniles may occasionally be found in coastal bays.

This species is readily identified by the tail fin shape, which has the upper lobe broad and deeply notched, giving the appearance of a double tail. The dorsal fin is set well forward and is closer to the commencement of the pectoral than the ventral fins. Both jaws carry sharp, triangular teeth of similar size which immediately separates the school shark from the gummy shark with its smooth and flattened teeth.

The school shark can reach 2 m and 60 kg but is commonly much smaller. School sharks can live more than 40 years and a tagged fish had grown only 18 cm in over 35 years at liberty.

Fishing: The school shark is frequently taken with gummy sharks and other cool water reef species on the deeper reefs of southern waters. Standard snapper rigs and baits of fish flesh, squid and cuttlefish will take the majority of school sharks. A trace is recommended as the school shark can easily bite through monofilament lines. Smaller specimens can be taken on similar shallower reefs in larger bays and estuaries. A trace is recommended.

The school shark is excellent eating but should be kept cool as, like all sharks, a build up of ammonia can accumulate in the flesh if the fish is not well handled.

Rigs and Tactics:

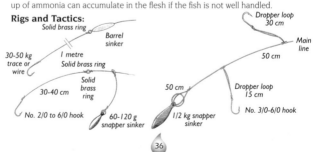

SHARK, WHITE POINTER

Scientific name: Carcharodon carcharias. Also known as Great white shark, white shark, white death.

Description: The white pointer shark is a large and extremely dangerous species and the star of the Jaws movies which has lead to the misguided destruction of many harmless sharks. However, the white pointer is responsible for more attacks on humans than any other species. The white pointer is a heavy set species, reaching 6.4 m and more than 1200 kilograms. As in most shark species, males are smaller and easily identified by the claspers which assist in copulation. The white pointer shark has a conical snout, long gill slits and extremely sharp, serrated triangular teeth. The colour is generally grey to dark grey above with a white belly. The white pointer prefers oceanic waters and does not often move close inshore, except to breed or to follow seal colonies when pups are produced. They are more commonly found inshore along the south coast or Tasmania.

SPOTTED, WOBBEGONG

Scientific name: Orectolobus maculatus. Also known as Common catshark, tassel shark.

Description: The spotted wobbegong shark inhabits coastal and estuarine reefs of cooler waters, being most common in NSW. Wobbegongs are easily identified by the numerous fleshy tentacle-like appendages around the front of the rounded head.

This species is identified by two wart-like protrusions above each eye and the large pale-edged spots which resemble the large eyes on the dorsal surface. The spotted wobbegong can reach 3.2 m and is harmless except when disturbed by divers. There have been some instances where large wobbegongs have felt trapped in small caves by divers and attacked. They are good eating.

SKATE, MELBOURNE

Scientific name: *Raja whitleyi*. Also known as Whitley's skate, great skate.

Description: All skates lack the venomous spines of the stingrays and stingarees. This species is the largest, reaching 50 kg and 1.7 metres. The Melbourne skate is common in shallow coastal waters but is most commonly caught in trawls.

The upper surface is brownish-grey and flecked with white. The undersurface of the triangular snout is a similar colour. In the smaller thornback skate (Raja lemprieri) which is also found in Victoria, the underside of the snout is black. The upper surface is covered with sharp denticles with the largest on either side of the midline whereas the thornback skate has a row of prominent spines along the backbone.

Fishing: Baits must be fished on the bottom with standard bottom fishing rigs over sand or other soft bottom. Baits include squid, prawns, cut fish or worm baits.

In common with all dorsally compressed species, skates put up an extremely powerful, if unspectacular fight. They can sit on the bottom until the frustrated angler breaks the line.

Skates are very good eating, with the wings being very tasty and passable 'mock' scallops can be made with a round cookie cutter.

Rigs and Tactics:

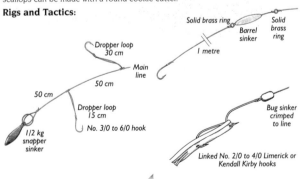

SNAPPER

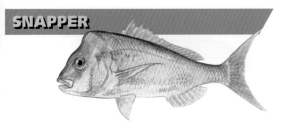

Scientific name: *Pagrus auratus.* (formerly Chrysophrys auratus) Also known as schnapper, Pink snapper and pinkie. With increasing size known as Cockney bream, red bream, squire, snapper and ultimately 'old man snapper' with the characteristic hump.

Description: A truly stunning and highly sought after species, the snapper can have iridescent pink to burnished copper colouration with bright blue spots from the lateral line upwards which are brightest in younger fish. A hump on the head and nose area develops in some fish and is more likely in male fish. Snapper are relatively slow growing and mature at 29 to 35 cm and four to five years of age. Snapper numbers have been affected by both commercial and recreational overfishing.

Fishing: Snapper are traditionally taken on bottom paternoster rigs with the famous snapper lead. Snapper prefer the edges of reefs or broken ground and can be taken from the shore or as deep as 50 fathoms. Drifting over broken ground or drop-offs at the edges of reefs with just enough weight to bounce bottom will find fish and repeated drifts will pick up more fish. Like many reef species, snapper form schools of similar sized fish, with the size of the school decreasing with larger fish.

In late winter on the east coast, snapper move inshore to feed on spawning cuttlefish and large fish can be taken from the rocks on cuttlefish baits.

Quality snapper can be taken by sinking a bait under a feeding school of tailor, salmon or small mackerel, feeding on uneaten baitfish. Snapper are a magnificent fighting fish and are excellent eating, but do not freeze particularly well.

Rigs and Tactics:

No. 3/0 to 6/0 hook-Suicide or Viking pattern

Dropper loop 30 cm

Main line

50 cm

50 cm

Dropper loop 15 cm

No. 3/0 to 6/0 hook

1/2 kg snapper sinker

Solid brass ring

Solid brass ring

Main line

No. 2/0 to 8/0 hook   60-120 g snapper sinker

No. 3/0 to 5/0 Suicide hook

Small octopus

Bug sinker crimped to line

Linked No. 2/0 to 4/0 Limerick or Kendall Kirby hooks

saltwater Species

SNAPPER, QUEEN

Scientific name: *Nemadactylus valenciennesi*. Also known as southern blue morwong.

Description: A handsome representative of the morwong family, the queen snapper is often a rich blue colour. There are distinctive yellow lines on the face and around the eyes and there is usually a large black blotch in the middle of the side of the fish. The queen snapper has the extended rays of the pectoral fin like many of the morwongs. The tail fin is deeply forked.

The queen snapper is found from inshore reefs to a depth of 240 m and has a preference for reef country.

SNAPPER, RED

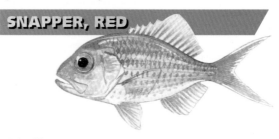

Scientific name: Centroberyx gerrardi. Also known as Bight redfish.

Description: The red snapper is most commonly a species of deeper reefs in cooler southern waters which may range from shallow reefs to more than 300 metres. A handsome species very similar to the smaller nannygai but is able to be separated by having 6 dorsal fin spines versus 7 in the nannygai.

The red snapper has a distinctive white line along the lateral line and white margins on the fins.

The head is also less rounded than in the nannygai. The eye is generally red but can fade to red-silver after death. The red snapper can reach 66 cm, but is more common at 40 – 45 centimetres. It is found singly in larger sizes or in small groups when smaller.

SNOOK

Scientific name: *Sphyraena novaehollandiae*. Also known as Short finned sea pike, sea pike, short finned barracuda.

Description: The snook is a very long and skinny southern relative of the barracuda. It is easily separated from the barracuda by its southern range and the first dorsal fin which commences well behind the end of the pectoral fin, while the first dorsal commences at the tip of the pectoral fin in barracuda. The snook is similar to the long finned sea pike but most easily separated by the snook's shorter anal fin, and its ventral fins which are set well behind the pectoral fin.

The snook reaches 1.1 m and 5 kilograms and is a highly regarded sportfish.

SWEEP, SEA

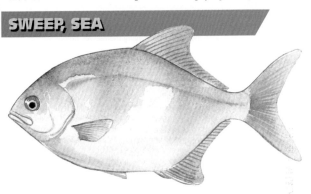

Scientific name: *Scorpis aequipinnis*. Also known as Sweep.

Description: The sea sweep is a deep bodied fish quite common on deeper reefs of the south coast and can also be found inshore, especially in schools when young. The sea sweep is generally slate grey in colour. It may have two darker grey patches on the upper body above the back edge of the pectoral fin and also the back part of the dorsal fin. This species has a prominent lobe to the first dorsal ray whereas the similar silver sweep (Scorpis lineolatus) has a flat dorsal fin profile. The mouth extends to the middle of the eye in the sea sweep and only to the front edge of the eye in the silver sweep.

The sea sweep can reach 61 cm and more than 3.5 kilograms.

TAILOR

Scientific name: *Pomatomus saltatrix*. Also known as Tailer, chopper, bluefish (USA), elf (South Africa), skipjack.

Description: The tailor is a renowned predatory species best known for its relatively small but extremely sharp teeth. The tailor has a moderately forked tail, and a bluish to blue-green back which changes to more silvery and white on the belly. The eye can be yellow. The fins vary in colour but the tail fin is usually darker than the others.

Juvenile tailor are found in estuaries and embayments. Larger tailor move to the beaches and inshore reefs at between 25 – 35 centimetres. Tailor undergo a spawning migration, finishing at Fraser Island in Queensland. Tailor can reach 10 kg with any fish over 5 kg being rightly claimed as a prize and fish over 1.5 kg being large. Tailor are voracious feeders, with individual fish gorging themselves before regurgitating to continue in a feeding frenzy.

Fishing: Tailor are a highly prized species which readily takes a bait, fights hard and, if bled immediately after capture make fine eating. Tailor can be taken from boat or shore, on lure, fly or bait and by anglers of any skill level.

The most common bait and rig would be a whole pilchard bait on a gang hook rig. In the surf and where casting distance is required, a sliding sinker rig works best, with a star or spoon sinker on a dropper trace doing well. In estuaries, from a boat, or in calmer surf, an unweighted or minimally weighted bait provides by far the best results. Tailor readily feed high in the water column and avidly attack a floating bait. Another rig which works well is to use a nearly filled plastic bubble to gain casting distance without rapidly sinking the bait. Tailor bite best at dusk and dawn.

Tailor smoke very well and are fair eating when fresh which is improved if fish are immediately bled. The flesh of the tailor is fairly oily and bruises easily. Tailor makes a quality cut bait.

Rigs and Tactics:

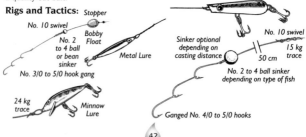

Stopper

No. 10 swivel

Bobby
Float

No. 2
to 4 ball
or bean
sinker

Metal Lure

No. 3/0 to 5/0 hook gang

24 kg
trace

Minnow
Lure

No. 10 swivel

Sinker optional
depending on
casting distance

15 kg
trace

50 cm

No. 2 to 4 ball sinker
depending on type of fish

Ganged No. 4/0 to 5/0 hooks

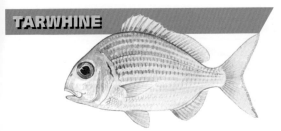

Scientific name: *Rhabdosargus sarba*. Also known as Silver bream.

Description: The tarwhine is similar to the various bream species but differs in a few key areas. The tarwhine has a number of thin golden or brown stripes running the length of the otherwise silver body. The nose of the tarwhine is blunt and there are 11 or 12 anal rays whereas bream have 9 or fewer. The fins other than the dorsal fin are generally bright yellow or yellow-orange and the tarwhine has a black lining to its gut cavity. Tarwhine are common in inshore and estuarine areas and may be found on offshore reefs on occasions. Tarwhine form schools, especially in smaller sizes. Tarwhine can reach 80 cm and more than 3 kg but they are most commonly caught at a few hundred grams.

Fishing: Tarwhine can be voracious feeders, taking a wide variety of foods. Tarwhine readily take cut flesh, bluebait, whitebait and parts of pilchard but many more are caught on prawn, pipi, worm, nipper or squid baits. Tarwhine are also occasionally taken on cabbage baits by luderick and drummer fishermen in NSW.

While tarwhine bite very hard, their relatively small mouth and frequent small size makes them nuisance bait pickers in many instances. Use a smaller hook for better results, but don't let the fish run with the bait too far as they can easily become gut hooked. In estuaries or shallow waters, a light running ball sinker rig works best while off the rocks or in deeper water, use as little weight and as light a rig as you can get away with. Tarwhine fight well for their size. They also make very good eating although they can have an iodine taste if not bled immediately and the guts and black stomach lining removed as soon as possible.

Rigs and Tactics:

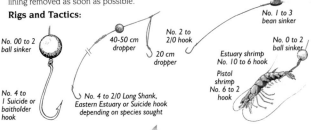

No. 00 to 2 ball sinker

No. 4 to 1 Suicide or baitholder hook

40-50 cm dropper

No. 2 to 2/0 hook

20 cm dropper

No. 4 to 2/0 Long Shank, Eastern Estuary or Suicide hook depending on species sought

No. 1 to 3 bean sinker

No. 0 to 2 ball sinker

Estuary shrimp No. 10 to 6 hook

Pistol shrimp No. 6 to 2 hook

saltwater Species

TREVALLY, SILVER

Scientific name: *Pseudocaranx dentex*. Also known as White trevally, skipjack trevally, skippy.

Description: A common schooling fish of cooler waters, the silver trevally is found in inshore areas but may be found near offshore cover. Juveniles are often encountered in estuaries and bays but larger fish can also be found in these areas on occasions. The fins may be yellow and a narrow yellow stripe is often found on these fish but most fish are silver with a blue-green or darker blue, and dark bands may be present. The silver trevally can reach 1 m and more than 10 kg but fish of 2 kg are much more common and in most areas, a fish of 5 kg is noteworthy. The mouth is relatively small, finishing well in front of the start of the eye and the lips are rubbery. There is an obvious black spot on the rear edge of the opercular (cheek) bone.

Fishing: Like all trevally, they can be good sport, especially on light line. Silver trevally can be taken on small lures such as small spoons, leadhead jigs and small minnow lures. They can be coaxed to take flies, particularly when berley is used with a school of fish. While silver trevally can feed on the surface, they prefer to feed on or near sandy or gravel bottoms and lures presented close to the bottom do best. Silver trevally are a better bait proposition, taking baits such as half pilchard, bluebait, whitebait, cut fish baits, squid, prawn, crab, pipi, nipper or cunjevoi depending on the food found in the area fished. Silver trevally respond well to berley.

Silver trevally can be taken on lines of 3 – 8 kg where they provide excellent sport. As they are a schooling fish which are not too prone to disperse if one fish escapes, persistence pays off with light line. Small silver trevally make excellent live baits, but size and bag limits must be followed. Silver trevally are fair eating, and must be bled on capture.

Rigs and Tactics:

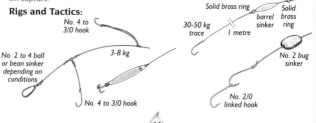

No. 4 to 3/0 hook

No. 2 to 4 ball or bean sinker depending on conditions

3-8 kg

No. 4 to 3/0 hook

Solid brass ring

30-50 kg trace

1 metre

barrel sinker

Solid brass ring

No. 2 bug sinker

No. 2/0 linked hook

TRUMPETER, BASTARD

Scientific name: *Latridopsis forsteri*. Also known as Moki, copper moki, silver trumpeter.

Description: The bastard trumpeter is a common species on inshore reefs of southern Victoria. This species can reach 65 cm and more than 4 kilograms. In smaller sizes, it forms schools but larger specimens are more solitary and can be found in waters beyond 30 fathoms.

The mouth is small and set low down. The back and upper flanks are silvery-brown with a pattern of close-set slender yellow or white lines running along the body. The fins are brownish in colour and the edges of the pectoral, dorsal and the forked tail fin are black.

Fishing: The bastard trumpeter is occasionally taken by anglers on baits of prawn, squid, cockles or worms. The small mouth means that a smaller, long-shanked hook will increase catches, as will berley. Standard snapper rigs with smaller hooks will take this fish.

The bastard trumpeter is more frequently taken by spearfishermen. The bastard trumpeter is excellent eating.

Rigs and Tactics:

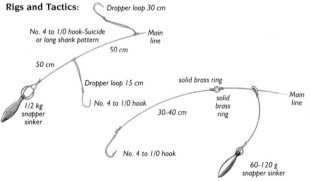

Dropper loop 30 cm

No. 4 to 1/0 hook-Suicide or long shank pattern

Main line

50 cm

50 cm

Dropper loop 15 cm

1/2 kg snapper sinker

No. 4 to 1/0 hook

solid brass ring

solid brass ring

Main line

30-40 cm

No. 4 to 1/0 hook

60-120 g snapper sinker

TRUMPETER, TASMANIAN

Scientific name: *Latris lineata*. Also known as Striped trumpeter, common trumpeter, stripey.

Description: The Tamanian trumpeter is is a medium to large species reaching 1.2 m and up to 25 kg, although the largest fish are found in deep waters. Overfishing has depleted stocks of the Tasmanian trumpeter on inshore reefs, where mainly juveniles are now found.

The Tasmanian trumpeter has three distinctive brownish stripes along the sides. The Tasmanian trumpeter is easily separated from the similar morwongs as it lacks the extended 'fingers' on the pectoral fins. The fins are dusky and may have a yellow or reddish tinge. The mouth is large and the lips quite blubbery.

TUNA, SOUTHERN BLUEFIN

Scientific name: *Thunnus maccoyii*. Also known as SBT, southern blue, bluefin, bluey, tunny.

Description: The southern bluefin tuna is a heavily built and very highly prized species which prefers open oceanic waters, especially in larger sizes. The southern bluefin tuna can grow to greater than 150 kg but is most commonly caught well below this size. Small southern bluefin can be found in inshore waters and weigh from 3 – 25 kg, with the average size generally increasing as you move eastwards along the southern coast. Southern bluefin tuna have been overexploited by commercial fishing operations, especially on the high seas. The commercial overexploitation has lead to the development of extensive aquaculture. Southern bluefin tuna can be identified by their heavy bodies, and the short pectoral fins which do not extend to the second dorsal. The dorsal and anal lobes are also short as opposed to the yellowfin with its scythe-like lobes in larger fish. The finlets at the rear of the body are edged with black and the caudal keels on the wrist of the tail are conspicuously yellow, especially in the sizes normally encountered by recreational fishers. They are a first rate sportfish and make sublime eating.

TUNA, STRIPED

Scientific name: *Katsuwonis pelamis*. Also known as Skipjack, skipjack tuna, stripey, aku.

Description: The striped tuna is a small, thickset schooling species which rapidly tapers at the rear of the body to a smallish tail. Sometimes misidentified as a bonito, but striped tuna lack the obvious teeth of the bonito and have no stripes on the upper flanks or back. Instead, the 4 – 6 horizontal stripes on the striped tuna are found on the lower flanks and belly. The area under and around the pectoral fin lacks stripes. The striped tuna can reach more than 15 kg, but in Australia any fish over 10 kg is exceptional and the average size is between 1 and 6 kilograms. Schools of striped tuna can be massive and may contain hundreds of tonnes of fish. This species forms the basis of significant commercial fisheries in many countries.

Fishing: Striped tuna are mainly taken on lures trolled or cast from boats, deep shores or jetties which extend to deeper water. Many striped tuna are taken on heavy cord lines and Smiths jigs to be used as bait or berley. Striped tuna provide excellent sport on lighter lines as they are very hard fighting speedsters.

Most bright lures which work well at around 5 knots will take striped tuna, with Christmas tree style lures working well. Slices, slug lures, feather jigs, small poppers and medium sized flies also take good numbers of fish, although striped tuna can be finicky about size and action type of lures at times.

Striped tuna can be taken on pilchards, cut baits or squid, especially if a berley trail excites the fish. Larger fish can take small live baits. Striped tuna have very dark red meat which is quite strongly flavoured but is suitable for smoking, salting and canning. It bled and chilled immediately they are fair eating. However, striped tuna are excellent live baits for large pelagics and their cut flesh makes a first rate bait or berley where their oil rich red flesh attracts most species.

Rigs and Tactics:

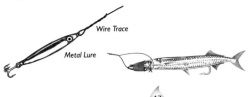

Wire Trace

Metal Lure

TUNA, YELLOWFIN

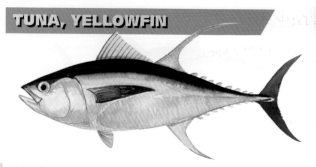

Scientific name: *Thunnus albacares*. Also known as Allison tuna, yellowfin or 'fin, ahi.

Description: The yellowfin tuna is a beautiful, powerful and challenging species which prefers warmer currents but may move inshore where deep water comes close to the coast. The yellowfin tuna is easily separated from other tunas by the scythe-like dorsal and anal lobes in adult fish.

The pectoral fin is long and extends to the commencement of the second dorsal fin.

Small yellowfin have short dorsal and anal lobes, but have whitish bars down the sides which may disappear after death. The liver of yellowfin tuna is smooth as opposed to the ridged liver of the bigeye. The caudal keels (ridges) on the wrist of the tail are also dusky and never yellow as in the southern bluefin tuna.

Yellowfin tuna can reach more than 200 kg in other parts of the world, but in Australia fish over 100 kg are magnificent and most fish are between 2 and 50 kilograms. They are excellent eating.

Rigs and Tactics:

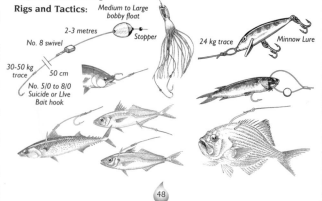

Medium to Large bobby float

2-3 metres
Stopper

No. 8 swivel

30-50 kg trace
50 cm

No. 5/0 to 8/0 Suicide or Live Bait hook

24 kg trace
Minnow Lure

WAREHOU

Scientific name: *Seriolella brama*. Also known as Silver warehou, blue warehou, snotty trevally, snot-nose trevalla, snot-gall, snotty.

Description: The warehou is a deep water schooling reef fish that can make inshore migrations, especially during winter. The warehou is common in Victorian waters. The warehou grows to 7 kg with smaller specimens more likely to be encountered in the shallower waters more commonly fished by recreational anglers. The warehou is best identified by the rounded head and the dark patch behind the head and above the pectoral fin, but this fades with death. Warehou look similar to silver trevally but lack the scutes along the side near the tail. The warehou has a thick mucous coating and translucent nose area which gives rise to its less appetising common names like snotty.

Fishing: Larger warehou are taken with heavy rigs fished on deep reefs. It requires heavy tackle and patience to find warehou. Many more fish are taken on inshore migrations when large schools of fish 0.5 – 1 kg can be taken in good numbers. Local information is invaluable in locating known hotspots and times of aggregation.

Best baits include prawns, crabs, squid and cut flesh baits. When warehou are inshore, these baits are fished on fairly light multiple hook rigs. Warehou will occasionally take small lures but jigs tipped with bait and vertically jigged or bobbed near the bottom work better.

Warehou are a common commercial catch which is gaining acceptance in the marketplace. The flesh is soft and does not freeze well. Warehou should be bled and cleaned soon after capture.

Rigs and Tactics:

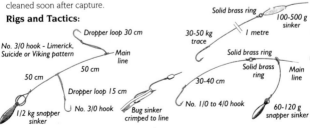

WHITING, GRASS

Scientific name: *Haletta semifasciata*. Also known as Rock whiting, blue rock whiting, weed whiting, stranger.

Description: Although the grass whiting vaguely resembles other whitings, this species is more closely related to the wrasses or parrotfish as it possesses fused teeth. It is a relatively common species which prefers seagrass habitats but may be found on nearby sand patches or shallow reefs. There is a single long dorsal fin compared with two dorsal fins for whiting. The grass whiting can reach 41 centimetres.

There is vastly different colouring between males and females, with males a brighter bluish green with a black blotch towards the rear of the dorsal fin. Females and juveniles have pale greenish-brown backs which fade to brown after death. There is a distinctive blue blotch around the anus.

WHITING, SOUTHERN SCHOOL

Scientific name: *Sillago bassensis*. Also known as silver whiting

Description: The whitings can be extremely difficult to tell apart and the southern school whiting is one of the more difficult species to separate. The eastern school whiting (Sillago flindersi) only overlaps its range in Western Port in Victoria and is more heavily marked on the dorsal surface. The bars or streaks on the top of the southern school whiting may be very faint and a light orange or sandy brown colour. Under the water these streaks are very difficult to see. After death these bars may fade entirely giving a silver appearance. There is no spot at the base of the pectoral fin which separates the southern school whiting from all other similar species other than the yellow-fin whiting which has yellow to orange ventral fins. The southern school whiting is found on inshore sandy areas and will follow the tide onto sand flats and beaches. Although they are taken by recreational fishers in shallow waters, they can be taken on deeper sand bank and are trawled by commercial fishers to a depth of 55 metres. The southern school whiting can reach a very pleasing 36 centimetres.

WHITING, KING GEORGE

Scientific name: *Sillaginodes punctata*. Also known as Spotted whiting, KG, KGW.

Description: The King George whiting is the largest and most sought after whiting species in Australia reaching 67 cm and more than 2 kg, with the largest specimens found in oceanic waters. Juveniles spend time near sea grass beds inshore or in estuaries before moving to more open waters. King George whiting prefer sand patches near weed beds, gravel or broken reef country with water up to 10 m in depth being the most productive. King George whiting are readily identified by the typical whiting down-turned mouth and the distinctive dark brown or red-brown spots and broken dashes along the body.

Fishing: The King George whiting is a magnificent and hard fighting whiting species. Smaller fish succumb most readily to baits of prawn, pipi, mussel, crab, yabbie and worms. These baits are fished on light line with minimal weight near the edges of drop-offs or sand patches in sea grass beds or reef areas. Larger specimens can be caught on blue sardines or whitebait. The largest King George whiting are taken on reef fishing rigs near reefs in depths up to 30 metres.

Berley can work well, but can also attract bait pickers which are a nuisance. The best King George whiting experts adopt a mobile approach, fishing sometimes tiny sand patches near heavy cover and moving on if there are no bites in a few minutes. King George whiting are rarely taken on jigs, flies or other small lures generally intended for flathead or flounder. The King George whiting is magnificent eating, combining the meat quality of all whiting in a size large enough that generous boneless fillets can be obtained.

Rigs and Tactics.

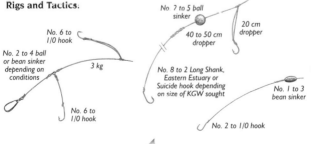

No. 6 to 1/0 hook

No. 2 to 4 ball or bean sinker depending on conditions

3 kg

No. 6 to 1/0 hook

No. 7 to 5 ball sinker

40 to 50 cm dropper

20 cm dropper

No. 8 to 2 Long Shank, Eastern Estuary or Suicide hook depending on size of KGW sought

No. 1 to 3 bean sinker

No. 2 to 1/0 hook

WHITING, SAND

Scientific name: *Sillago ciliata*. Also known as Silver whiting, summer whiting, blue nose whiting.

Description: The sand whiting is a common species of inshore and tidal sandy areas. The sand whiting can reach 47 cm and around a kilogram. It is readily identified by the lack of a silver stripe along the side and the dusky blotch at the base of the pectoral fin. Large sand whiting are sometimes confused with bonefish, but all whitings have two dorsal fins while the bonefish has one.

Fishing: A scrappy little fighter which gives a good account of itself for its size. The sand whiting is a terrific light line quarry and fine tackle will greatly increase the number of strikes. Use the absolute minimum weight to either reach the bottom or to keep the bait from swinging wildly in current or wave wash. Sand whiting will take a moving bait and a slow retrieve will attract fish. A long trace behind a small ball sinker is the preferred rig. As whiting have a small mouth, a long shank hook around size 6 – 2 is recommended. Either putting red tubing or a few red beads above the hook works very well.

The sand whiting feeds on yabbies, pipis, prawns and especially beach, squirt or blood worms and all these make terrific baits. On a rising tide, sand whiting can be caught in very shallow water of only a few centimetres, while on a falling tide, fish the deeper edges of gutters or drop-offs but success is less assured. Sand whiting are a delicate, sweet flavoured fish often highly priced in restaurants but there can be a number of fine bones.

Rigs and Tactics:

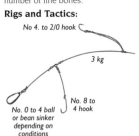

No 4. to 2/0 hook

3 kg

No. 8 to 4 hook

No. 0 to 4 ball or bean sinker depending on conditions

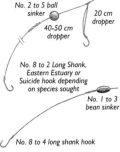

No. 2 to 5 ball sinker

20 cm dropper

40-50 cm dropper

No. 8 to 2 Long Shank, Eastern Estuary or Suicide hook depending on species sought

No. I to 3 bean sinker

No. 8 to 4 long shank hook

WRASSE, MAORI

Scientific name: *Opthalmolepis lineolatus*. Also known as southern Maori wrasse, Maori.

Description: An attractive wrasse which can reach 41 cm, but is more often encountered at a smaller, bait stealing size. This species is found on inshore, or more often offshore reefs throughout its range. The males and females are different in appearance. The males have a black stripe along the body below the mid line. While both sexes have a prominent orange brown top to the body, the male has a number of bright blue spots through this area. Both male and female Maori wrasse have a number of small blue stripes on the head. The belly is yellow or creamy yellow and is below a wide white stripe down the side of the fish.

Fishing: The small mouth of this species and the fact that it occupies a similar area to more highly valued reef species such as snapper, morwong and dhufish means that the Maori wrasse is not highly regarded by anglers. The Maori wrasse can be taken on most baits, including on bait jigs when they are on inshore bait grounds. The Maori wrasse is generally used as a cut bait, but they make a quite acceptable live bait, being hardy and attractive to fish like Samson fish, kingfish and big snapper.

YELLOWTAIL

Scientific name: *Trahurus novaezelandiae*. Also known as Yellowtail scad, scad, yakka, bung, chow.

Description: The yellowtail is a common schooling forage fish of inshore estuaries, bays or inshore oceanic waters. The yellowtail reaches 33 cm but is most commonly encountered at between 18 and 25 centimetres. Yellowtail have scutes (large scales) which extend from the back of the head.

Fishing: Gear can be as basic as a handline with 4 kg line and a size 12 long-shanked hook. One or no split shot completes the rig. Yellowtail will take most baits, but the most common baits are small pieces of cut bait, prawn, squid, mince meat, heart or mullet roe. Yellowtail respond very well to berley, with bran, pollard or commercial berleys working well. Yellowtail make very good whole dead baits with fairly oily flesh, but they are arguably the best live bait available.

BASS, AUSTRALIAN

Scientific name: *Macquaria novemaculeata*. Also known as Bass, Australian perch.

Description: The Australian bass is a handsome fish which can reach more than 4 kg in impoundments, but any fish from the rivers over 2 kg is an extremely noteworthy capture. Males are smaller than females and a large male will be up to 1 kilogram.

The Australian bass is easily confused with the similar estuary perch. Even experts can confuse the two species, but they can be most easily separated by the forehead profile which is straight or slightly rounded in the bass and is concave or slightly indented in the estuary perch. Australian bass must have salt water to breed and the increased construction of weirs and dams on coastal streams has had a significant impact on bass numbers.

Fishing: The Australian bass is arguably the best light tackle sportfish of temperate waters in Australia. They have a close affinity for structure and will dash out from their snag to grab a lure, bait or fly and madly dash back into cover, busting off the unwary. While not as powerful as mangrove jacks of tropical waters, they are spectacular sport in their own right.

Australian bass can be extremely aggressive, feeding on fish, shrimps, prawns, insects, lizards and small snakes that may fall into the water.

Australian bass are more active at dusk, dawn or at night. Fishing on a summer's evening is almost unbeatable, with surface lures or popping bugs on a fly rod producing spectacular strikes from dusk and well into the night. Many lures work well and bass anglers have massive collections of surface lures, shallow divers, deep divers, soft plastics, spinnerbaits and special lures in every conceivable pattern and colour. Many baits work well for bass, with live baits being best. A live shrimp or prawn drifted under a quill float will almost guarantee a response from any bass, but this includes very small fish which may be gut hooked if the hook is set too late. Live fish such as poddy mullet also work well, as do grasshoppers, worms and live cicadas during summer.

Rigs and Tactics:

Freshwater popper

Deep Diving Minnow

Balance with lead shot

2-3 metres

Stopper

Float

No. 6 to 4 fly hook

CARP

Scientific name: *Cyprinus carpio*. Also known as European carp, Euro, common carp, koi, blubber lips, mud sucker. Lightly scaled individuals known as mirror carp and those with no or very few scales are known as leather carp.

Description: The carp has a relatively small, downward pointing mouth surrounded by two pairs of barbels, with the second pair more prominent. The first spines in the dorsal and anal fins are strongly serrated. Scales may be present, in rows and of a larger size, or almost entirely absent.

The decorative koi is a variety of carp and, if released, can breed to wild strain fish capable of much more rapid growth and reproduction. Carp can hybridise with common goldfish (*Carassius auratus*).

CATFISH, EEL-TAILED

Scientific name: *Tandanus tandanus*. Also known as Tandan, freshwater jewfish, dewfish, freshwater catfish, kenaru, cattie, tandan catfish.

Description: A largely nocturnal species with smooth skin and a robust eel-like tail. The eel-tailed catfishes' intimidating looks mask a terrific eating and hard fighting fish.

The eel-tailed catfish possesses stout and poisonous spines on the dorsal and pectoral fins.

The poison is stronger in juvenile catfish for, as the fish grows, the channel along the spine where the poison passes grows over and the spikes become less dangerous in animals over about 20 centimetres. However, the small fish hide in weeds during the day and can spike unwary waders. Immerse the wound in hot water and seek medical advice if swelling or persistent pain cause continued discomfort. Catfish take worms, shrimp, grasshoppers and mudeyes. They fight hard and dirty.

COD, MURRAY

Scientific name: *Maccullochella peelii peelii.* Also known as Cod, goodoo, green fish, codfish, ponde.

Description: The Murray cod is the largest Australian freshwater fish, reaching 1.8 m and 113 kilograms. Cod grow an average of 1 kg per year in rivers and 2 kg per year in larger dams. Has prominent mottling on body, reducing towards a white or cream belly. Fin borders except pectoral fins are white. Differs from similar trout cod in having lower jaw equal or longer than upper jaw, more prominent mottling and heavier tail wrist. Murray cod also prefer more sluggish water than trout cod.

Fishing: Murray cod are the largest predator in many inland waters. They take large lures, especially deep divers cast to snags or drop-offs in larger, slower rivers or dams. Murray cod are now a legitimate target for keen fly fishers. Murray cod reward patience, as a lure repeatedly cast to cod holding cover, or to a following fish will often eventually evoke a strike. As Murray cod are ambush feeders, large or flashy lures often work best.

Murray cod are best known for taking a wide range of baits including live fish (where permitted), bardi grubs, yabbies, worms, ox heart and even scorched starlings. Murray cod are very good eating, especially under 10 kilograms. Anglers should only take as many cod as they need.

Rigs and Tactics: No. 1 to 4 bean sinker

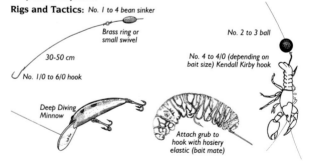

Brass ring or small swivel

30-50 cm

No. 1/0 to 6/0 hook

Deep Diving Minnow

No. 2 to 3 ball

No. 4 to 4/0 (depending on bait size) Kendall Kirby hook

Attach grub to hook with hosiery elastic (bait mate)

EEL, LONG-FINNED

Scientific name: *Anguilla reinhardtii*. Also known as Freshwater eel, eel, spotted eel.

Description: Eels are fascinating animals which are often loathed but play an important part in culling older or sick fish, birds or anything else they can catch. Australian eels are thought to spawn in the Coral Sea. Juvenile eels as elvers migrate great distances up rivers and can travel overland over wet grass and can negotiate large dams walls. Long-finned eels can spend more than 10 years in fresh waters until the urge to move downstream takes the adult eels.

The long-finned eel is much larger than the short-finned eel (*Anguilla australis*) and has the dorsal fin extending well forward of the anal fin. The head is broad and the lips fleshy. Colour varies with the environment but, except when migrating to the sea, is brown or olive-green with a lighter belly.

Fishing: The long-finned eel is often taken while fishing for other fish. They fight extremely hard and can be mean enough to try to bite the hand which tries to unhook it. The long-finned eel can demonstrate knot tying tricks when hooked. These eels are opportunistic feeders and can take live baits larger than the 10% of the body length which legend believes applies. Worms, grubs, live fish or cut baits will take eels, but liver and beef heart are irresistible. Long-finned eels can reach over 2 m and 20 kg, although divers claim much larger sizes in some dams. Eels make good eating, especially when smoked, although many Australians are strongly prejudiced against them. Large eels gain a top price in China, whereas smaller eels are more popular in Japan.

Rigs and Tactics:

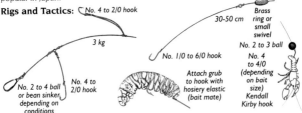

No. 4 to 2/0 hook

3 kg

No. 2 to 4 ball or bean sinker depending on conditions

No. 4 to 2/0 hook

No. 1 to 4 bean sinker

30-50 cm

Brass ring or small swivel

No. 2 to 3 ball

No. 1/0 to 6/0 hook

Attach grub to hook with hosiery elastic (bait mate)

No. 4 to 4/0 (depending on bait size) Kendall Kirby hook

PERCH, GOLDEN

Scientific name: *Macquaria ambigua*. Also known as Golden, callop, yellowbelly, Murray perch.

Description: The golden perch is a deep bodied fish which becomes more heavily set as it gets larger. Fish over 5 kg resemble a football, with a tail and a small moderately tapered head with a distinctly concave forehead. The lower jaw extends slightly beyond the upper jaw.

The colour varies with the water quality, ranging from pale green to almost cream out of very muddy western waters to deep green and with obvious golden overtones, particularly in the throat and belly region. There are two distinctive extended filaments on the ventral fins. Golden perch are most commonly encountered in the 1 – 2 kg range especially in rivers. However, the extremely successful stocking in Queensland, New South Wales and to a lesser extent Victorian impoundments has seen a huge increase in the number of 5 – 10 kg fish being caught with the odd fish to 15 kg being reported.

Fishing: The natural rivers where golden perch were once extremely common no longer ever run clear through poor land use and de-snagging. In these rivers, golden perch are almost exclusively

a bait proposition, except in the upper reaches or near barrages where lures can be used. Baits include worms, yabbies, shrimps, bardi and wood grubs and less common baits such as kangaroo meat or liver.

However, fishing for golden perch has exploded in popularity in impoundments. Bait fishing includes bobbing with yabbies near drowned timber or sight fishing with shrimps or live fish to cruising fish on the edge of weed beds, along rock walls or on drop-offs near points where this species positions itself to ambush prey. Lure fishing is now the most popular method of fishing for golden perch. Golden perch often follow lures, so a slight pause near the end of the retrieve will often entice a strike and working the rod while trolling is similarly more successful.

Rigs and Tactics:

No. 1 4 bean sinker
Brass ring or small swivel
30-50 cm
No. 4/0 to 3/0 hook

No. 4 to 2/0 hook
No. 2 to 4 ball or bean sinker depending on conditions
No. 4 to 2/0 hook

3 kg
Attach grub to hook with hosiery elastic (bait mate)

No. 2 to 3 ball
No. 4 to 4/0 (depending on bait size)
Kendall Kirby hook

PERCH, MACQUARIE

Scientific name: *Macquaria australasica*. Also known as Mountain perch, white eye perch, silvereye, macca, mountain perch, Murray bream, black perch, Macquaries.

Description: Macquarie perch are a distinctly perch-like fish reaching 3.5 kg but are commonly caught at half a kilogram. The Tallowa Dam and Kangaroo River population is rarely seen at even this size and many fish are around 15 to 20 centimetres. Although colouration can vary from black to blue-grey to light grey and piebald, the Macquarie perch has a distinctive white iris around the eye in all but black specimens. The mouth is relatively small and the lips are fairly obvious without being blubbery. The pectoral fins have two extended white filaments. Dartmouth Dam still contains large specimens.

PERCH, SILVER

Scientific name: *Bidyanus bidyanus*. Also known as grunter, black bream, bidyan, Murray perch, tcheri, freshwater bream, silver.

Description: The silver perch is a fine freshwater fish species, reaching 8 kg but most frequently encountered at between 0.3 kg and 1 kg, especially in impoundments. Larger silver perch frequently become omnivorous or almost entirely vegetarian, full of the green slimy weed which can seriously affect lure and bait fishing at some times of the year. The silver perch has a small head and small mouth, but they take large lures on occasions. As the fish grows, its head appears smaller than its body, especially in dams where fast growth rates leave a heavier body in larger fish. The rear margin of the small scales is dark grey or deep brown which gives a cross hatched appearance. The fish may grunt on capture but this is not as loud or as common as in other species. In dams especially, silver perch form schools of similar sized fish, with smaller schools of large fish.

Freshwater Species

REDFIN

Scientific name: *Perca fluviatilis*. Also known as English perch, European perch, redfin perch, reddie.

Description: The redfin has prominent scales and five to six prominent vertical stripes which may extend nearly to the belly. These stripes are less prominent in large fish. The dorsal fin is set well forward and when erect, resembles a small 'sail'. The ventral and anal fins are often very bright red or orange, often with a tinge of white at the ends. The tail fin can also be bright orange, or orange-yellow.

Redfin are often found around drowned timber, at drop-offs near points, or on submerged islands. Redfin prefer cooler water and in summer, the largest fish are almost always below the thermocline in dams or large river holes. Redfin are aggressive and prolific breeders. In impoundments they can stunt out, producing thousands of mature fish as small as 15 cm who consume everything and continue to reproduce. In other areas, they can reach 3 kg and provide excellent sport with a variety of techniques.

Fishing: In dams, one of the most successful techniques is to anchor among drowned timber and bob with bait or lures. With bait, a small ball sinker runs to the top of the hook which is baited with yabby, worm, cricket, grub or shrimp. Lures like the Baltic Bobber or the Buzz Bomb also work well.

In any case, the bait is lowered to the bottom and vertically jigged between 30 cm and a metre or so before being dropped to the bottom. Drifting baits near drowned timber in large holes in rivers or near drop-offs in rivers or dams is very succesful. Redfin are aggressive lure takers, with bladed, Celta type lures, diving lures, jigs and small Rapala minnows taking many fish.

Rigs and Tactics:

No. 00 to 4 bean sinker

30-50 cm

No. 4 to 2/0 hook

No. 2 to 3 ball

No. 0 to 4 ball or bean sinker depending on conditions

3 kg

No. 1/0 to 6/0 hook

No. 4 to 4/0 (depending on bait size) Kendall Kirby hook

No. 4 to 2/0 hook

Bladed Spinner

RIVER BLACKFISH

Scientific name: *Gadopsis marmoratus*. Also known as Blackfish, marble cod, slippery, slimy.

Description: The river blackfish is a small elongated native freshwater fish species which is easily identified by the pelvic fins which are reduced to two rays, each of which is divided and finger-like . The dorsal fin is very long and the tail fin is obviously rounded. The mouth is fairly large and the lower jaw is shorter than the upper jaw. This species has a distinctive marbled colouring and fish may vary in colour from almost black, to olive or light brown and there may be obvious purple overtones. The scales are small and the body feels very slimy, giving rise to several alternate common names. River blackfish do not appear to cohabit well with trout and prefer very snaggy waters. They are mainly nocturnal, laying up during the day in cover like hollow logs, which they also use to lay their eggs. The river blackfish can reach over 35 cm, although the two-spined species (which has obvious golden overtones) can reach nearly 5 kg in remote areas.

TROUT COD

Scientific name: *Maccullochella macquariensis*. Also known as Blue nose cod, bluenose, rock cod, blue cod.

Description: The trout cod is capable of reaching 16 kg and 800 mm but much more common at 1 – 2 kilograms. A handsome aggressive fish which puts up a terrific fight for its size, the trout cod has a slate grey to greenish blue colour and dashed markings. Trout cod, particularly juveniles have a prominent stripe through the eye and an overhanging upper jaw. The tail wrist is much narrower than in Murray cod. Trout cod are totally protected.

TROUT BROWN

Scientific name: *Salmo trutta*. Also known as Brownie, sea trout, Loch Leven trout.

Description: The brown trout is a handsome fish which can exhibit wide colour variations, partly dependent upon the environment in which the fish is found. Sea run fish and some lake dwelling fish are silver in colour with a few spots on the body. River fish in particular can have a beautiful golden sheen and large black spots on the upper body. There are frequently beautiful red spots, surrounded by a white halo below the lateral line which may be mixed with black spots.

In all fish, the dorsal fins has some spots but the tail fin has none or a few very faint spots. The tail fin is either square or very slightly indented, whereas the Atlantic salmon has an obvious indent or fork to the tail. The adipose fin is obvious and may be lobe-like in larger fish. The mouth is large and the jaws become hooked to a degree in males during spawning. The brown trout can reach 25 kg overseas, but in Australia they have been recorded to 14 kilograms.

Fishing: Brown trout are generally the most highly regarded Australian trout species, due to their large size and the skill which is needed to entice these fish to strike. Brown trout take a variety of foods which may include other trout, minnows, insect larvae, terrestrial insects, snails and worms.

Brown trout can be taken throughout the day, but the best times are dawn, dusk and at night. Night time is often the best in heavily fished waters, where a few wily, large, and often cannibalistic specimens can often be found.

Many brown trout are taken on fly, with nymphs, streamers, wet flies and dry flies all taking fish. Many brown trout feed heavily on yabbies or snails and imitations of these can be very productive. Brown trout generally prefer the slower waters of pools or the tails of pools in streams or deeper waters of lakes, moving into feeding stations during peak periods. Brown trout are also taken on a wide variety of lures, with favourites including lead head jigs, spoons, bladed lures like the Celta, and minnow or yabby lures. Brown trout take a variety of baits, with mudeyes, yabbies, minnows, grubs and worms being most successful. Brown trout will also take maggots, garden snails, corn, cheese, marshmallows and dog food on at least some occasions.

Rigs and Tactics:

No. 1 to 4 bean sinker

Brass ring or small swivel

30-50 cm

No. 6 to 2 hook

No. 6 to 8 long shank baitholder

2-3 kg main line

Minnow Lure

Cobra Pattern Lure eg. Tassie Devil

Fly fishing is successful

Scientific name: *Oncorhynchus mykiss.* (formerly Salmo gairdnerii). Also known as rainbow, 'bow, Steelhead.

Description: Rainbow trout possess the fleshy adipose fin of all salmonids behind the dorsal fin. The tail may be slightly forked but characteristically rainbow trout have spots over the entire tail and all of the body except the belly. A pink stripe along the body ranges from very pale in sea run and lake fish to crimson in river fish and those on their spawning run. Male rainbows develop a hooked lower jaw as spawning approaches. Females retain a more rounded head.

Fishing: Rainbow trout are generally easier to catch than brown trout but usually fight harder and often jump spectacularly. Rainbow trout are more mobile and will feed more freely in mid to shallow depths. This means that methods such as trolling are more successful, but rainbow trout can selectively feed on daphnia (water fleas) which can make them more difficult to catch.

Rainbow trout prefer faster water in streams than brown trout and will often take up station at the head of pools. Rainbow trout can be taken on fly, lure or bait. They take dry flies, wets, nymphs and streamer flies. Rainbow trout can be taken on bright colours and gaudy streamer flies can work well. Rainbow trout take all baits. A lightly weighted worm in streams or fairly close to the bank takes fish as do mudeyes fished under a bubble float or trolled with Cowbell trolling blades. Yabbies, grubs and live fish (where legal) take good catches.

Rigs and Tactics:

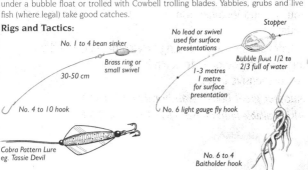

No. 1 to 4 bean sinker

Brass ring or small swivel

30-50 cm

No. 4 to 10 hook

No lead or swivel used for surface presentations

Stopper

Bubble float 1/2 to 2/3 full of water

1-3 metres
1 metre
for surface presentation

No. 6 light gauge fly hook

Cobra Pattern Lure
eg. Tassie Devil

No. 6 to 4
Baitholder hook

Waterproof VICTORIAN FISH GUIDE

THE DEFINITIVE GUIDE TO VICTORIA'S FISH SPECIES AND HOW TO CATCH THEM

Containing accurate fish illustrations, descriptions, and diagrams of the best rigs to catch each fish, this book is an invaluable reference for any angler, fresh or salt water, wanting to identify their catch.

You will find Victorian fish from both salt water and fresh water.

Whatever fish you're chasing in Victoria, you'll find the information you need to catch it and identify it in this comprehensive book.

Another great book by author, Frank Prokop.

Also available in this series: QLD, NSW and WA Fish Guide.

PO. Box 544, Croydon, Victoria 3136
Telephone (03) 9729 8788
Emal: sales@afn.com.au
Website: www.afn.com.au

ISBN 1865130753

9 781865 130750

J1204